Keto Bre

The Best 80 Low Carb Recipes For Optimal Ketosis & Weight Loss

Your Free Gifts

As a way of thanking you for the purchase, I'd like to offer you 2 complimentary gifts:

- **How To Get Through Any Weight Loss Plateau While On The Ketogenic Diet:** The title is self-explanatory; if you are struggling with getting off a weight loss plateau while on the Keto diet, you will find this free gift very eye opening on what has been ailing you. Grab your copy now by clicking/tapping here or simply enter http://bit.ly/2fantonpubketo into your browser.

- **5 Pillar Life Transformation Checklist:** This short book is about life transformation, presented in bit size pieces for easy implementation. I believe that without such a checklist, you are likely to have a hard time implementing anything in this book and any other thing you set out to do religiously and sticking to it for the long haul. It doesn't matter whether your goals relate to weight loss, relationships, personal finance, investing, personal development, improving communication in your family, your overall health, finances, improving your sex life, resolving issues in your relationship, fighting PMS successfully, investing, running a successful business, traveling etc. With a checklist like this one, you can bet that anything you do will seem a lot easier to implement until the end. Therefore, even if you don't continue reading this book, at least read the one thing that will help you in every other aspect of your life. Grab your copy [now by clicking/tapping here](http://bit.ly/2fantonfreebie) or simply enter http://bit.ly/2fantonfreebie into your browser. Your life will never be the same again (if you implement what's in this book), I promise.

PS: I'd like your feedback. If you are happy with this book, please leave a review on Amazon.

Introduction

Brighten your days while on keto by munching on breads, muffins, cookies, buns, waffles, bagels and much more without worrying about getting out of ketosis!

Have you committed to following a Ketogenic diet but are not yet committed to indulging in your favorite breads, cookies, buns and other baked goods? Are you **wondering if there is a way you can have bread and other delicious baked good**s without risking getting out of ketosis?

If you are, keep reading:

This book has **80 of the best (handpicked) recipes** that will support you throughout your journey to turning your body into an efficient fat burning machine!

If the thought, smell, sight or touch of bread waters your mouth and hijacks your mind such that saying no to such foods wears you down, don't worry, as this book will help you to have **your bread and eat it, literally!**

In this book, you will discover how to make keto friendly:

- Loafs
- **Flat bread**
- Buns/rolls
- **Waffles**

- Bread sticks

- **Crackers**

- Pizza crust

- **Muffins**

- Cookies

- **Bagels/donuts**

- And much more!

If you **thought being on keto meant you can't have all these baked goods, think again!** As you will find out, you can still enjoy a scrumptious meal without foregoing breads by making the bread recipes in this book!

And the good thing is that *the instructions are so easy; a 10 year old can follow them!* And you can have them for breakfast, lunch, dinner or snack; whatever tickles your fancy!

If <u>you love bread and baked goods and are on keto, don't waste another day wishing things were different; make any of the 80 recipes</u> in this book and you will find sticking to the keto diet effortless!

Table of Contents

Your Free Gifts _____ 2

Introduction _____ 4

Keto Loaf Recipes _____ 12

   Keto Coconut Bread _____ 12

   Keto Bread Loaf _____ 14

   Easy Paleo Keto Bread _____ 16

   Macadamia Nut Bread _____ 18

   Amazing Low Carb Keto Bread _____ 20

   Coconut Flour Mini Cheese Loaves _____ 22

   4-Ingredient Keto Almond Bread _____ 24

   Rosemary and Garlic Coconut Flour Bread _____ 25

   Zucchini Coconut Bread _____ 27

   Double Chocolate Zucchini Bread _____ 29

   Keto Collagen Protein Bread _____ 31

   Keto Bread _____ 33

   Lemon Blueberry Zucchini Bread _____ 35

   Keto Bread Low-Carb _____ 37

   The Best Keto Bread _____ 39

Flat Bread — 41

Keto Flatbread — 41

Easy Flatbread — 43

3-Ingredient Flatbread — 45

Rosemary Garlic Flatbread — 47

Coconut Flour Flatbread — 49

Low Carb Flatbread — 50

Low Carb Indian Flatbread — 52

Buns/Rolls — 54

Fluffy Keto Buns — 54

Best Keto Dinner Rolls — 56

Keto Burger Buns — 58

Keto Hamburger Buns — 60

Cheesy Keto Hamburger Buns — 62

Best Keto bread rolls — 64

Almond Flour Goji Buns — 66

Waffles — 68

Keto Waffles Stuffed with Cream Cheese — 68

Vanilla Keto Waffles — 70

Low Carb Waffles — 72

Keto Waffles with Blueberry Butter _____ 73

Protein Waffles _____ 75

Low Carb Waffles _____ 76

Bread Sticks _____ 77

Bread Sticks With Mozzarella Dough _____ 77

Keto Cheesy Breadsticks _____ 79

Cheesy Garlic Breadsticks _____ 81

Keto Breadstick Twists _____ 82

Cauliflower Breadsticks _____ 84

Low Carb Cheesy Breadsticks _____ 86

Low Carb Cauliflower Breadsticks _____ 88

Crackers _____ 90

Seed Crackers _____ 90

Almond Flour Crackers _____ 92

Spicy Ranch Crackers _____ 93

Cheese Thyme Keto Crackers _____ 95

Grain-Free Crackers _____ 97

Mustard Crackers _____ 99

Pizza Crust _____ 101

Almond Flour Pizza Crust _____ 101

Parmesan & Almond Flour Pizza Crust _____ 103

Low Carb Pizza Crust _____ 105

Zero Carb Pizza Crust _____ 107

Fathead Pizza Crust _____ 109

Gluten Free Tart Crust _____ 111

Pizza Bread Crust _____ 112

Bagels/Donuts _____ 114

Mozzarella Dough Bagels _____ 114

Easy Keto Bagel _____ 116

Keto Bagels _____ 117

Keto Sesame Bagels _____ 119

Low-Carb Bagels _____ 121

Fathead Bagel _____ 123

Muffins _____ 125

Keto Egg Muffins _____ 125

Almond and Coconut Muffin _____ 127

Salmon & Cream Cheese Mug Muffin _____ 129

Avocado & Bacon Muffins _____ 131

Low Carb English Muffin _____ 133

Lemon Poppy-seed Muffins _____135
One-Minute Keto Muffins _____137
Blueberry Muffin _____ 138

Cookies _____140

Thick and Fudgy Brownie Cookies _____ 140
Snowball Cookies _____ 142
Keto Chocolate Chunk Cookies _____ 144
Easy Almond Thins _____ 146
Keto No Bake Cookies _____147
Chocolate Coconut Cookies _____ 148
Keto Mug Bread _____ 150
Crockpot Zucchini Bread _____ 151
Cheesy Cauliflower Garlic Bread _____153
Low Carb Quick Bread _____155
Broccoli & Cheddar Keto Bread _____157

Conclusion_____158

Do You Like My Book & Approach To Publishing? _____159

1: First, I'd Love It If You Leave a Review of This Book on Amazon. _____159

2: Check Out My Other Keto Diet Books _____ 159

3: Let's Get In Touch _____ 161

4: Grab Some Freebies On Your Way Out; Giving Is Receiving, Right? _____ 162

5: Suggest Topics That You'd Love Me To Cover To Increase Your Knowledge Bank. _____ 162

PSS: Let Me Also Help You Save Some Money! _____ 163

Keto Loaf Recipes

Keto Coconut Bread

Yields 16 slices

Ingredients

1/4 teaspoon baking powder

1/4 teaspoon Salt

1/2 cup olive or coconut oil

1/2 cup coconut flour

7 large eggs

1/2 teaspoon xanthan gum, optional

Directions

1. Heat your oven to 355 degrees F. Meanwhile, crack the 7 eggs into a medium sized bowl and mix until well combined or for about 1 minute.

2. To the bowl with eggs, add in coconut flour, baking powder, salt, butter and xanthan gum and mix the ingredients until well incorporated.

3. As soon as the batter is very thick, get a parchment paper and line a loaf tin (8.5 by 5 inches). Pour the dough into the tin and use a spatula to level it evenly.

4. Bake the contents until a skewer inserted into the bread comes out clean, or for approximately 50 minutes.

5. Slice the loaf and keep it refrigerated for about 5 days or in a freezer for not more than 14 days.

Calories 95, Carbs 1g, Protein 3g, Fat 9g

Keto Bread Loaf

Yields 15 Slices

Ingredients

1/4 teaspoon cream of tartar

1/4 teaspoon salt

2/3 cup almond milk

1/2 teaspoon Xantan gum

1 1/2 teaspoons baking powder

1/4 cup melted butter, cooled or coconut oil

1/3 cup coconut flour

2 1/2 cups almond flour

5 large eggs

Sesame seeds for topping, optional

Directions

1. First heat your oven to 350 degrees F.

2. Meanwhile, line a 9 by 5 inch loaf pan with the parchment.

3. Mix together almond flour, coconut flour, xanthan gum, baking powder and salt in a bowl until well incorporated. Set the mixture aside.

4. Carefully separate the egg yolks from the egg whites and then beat the yolks for approximately 3 minutes. Add in butter and beat again until blended.

5. Now beat the egg yolks along with the cream of tartar until you get stiff peaks.

6. Mix together the flour mixture with the butter and the egg yolks mixture. Add in milk and beat until well blended.

7. Then fold in the egg white into the smooth mixture and move the batter into the parchment lined pan. Use a spatula to smooth the mixture.

8. At this point, bake the loaf mixture until cooked through, or for about 50 to 60 minutes. Insert a toothpick into the center of the loaf to check if it comes out clean.

9. Allow the bread to cool in the pan for another 10 minutes or so, then remove from the pan. Let it cool fully.

10. Serve or keep the bread refrigerated for about 7 days.

Calories: 167, Carbs: 5g, Protein: 6g, Fat: 14g,

Easy Paleo Keto Bread

Serves 8

Ingredients

12 large egg whites

5 tablespoons + 1 teaspoon coconut oil

1/4 teaspoon sea salt

2 teaspoons of baking powder, gluten-free

1/4 cup coconut flour

1 cup blanched almond flour

Optional Ingredients

1/4 teaspoon cream of tartar

1/4 teaspoon xanthan gum

1 1/2 tablespoons Erythritol

Directions

1. Heat your oven to 325 degrees F. Meanwhile, line a 8.5 by 4.5 inch loaf pan with parchment and let the paper hang over the sides for easier removal.

2. Mix together coconut flour, almond flour, sea salt, xanthan gum, baking powder and erythritol in a food processor. Pulse the mixture until well incorporated.

3. Add in the melted butter, pulse again until crumbly as you scrape the sides of the food processor as required.

4. Beat the cream of tartar and the egg whites in a large bowl until you obtain stiff peaks. Ensure that the bowl is large enough to accommodate the expanding egg whites.

5. To the food processor, add 1/2 of the stiff egg whites and now pulse a couple of times until well blended. Take care not to over-mix.

6. Pour the mixture into a bowl that has the egg whites and then carefully fold until the streaks have disappeared. Just fold gently to ensure the mixture is fluffy, but without stirring.

7. Move the batter to the loaf pan lined with parchment and smooth the top. Push the batter to the center so as to round the top of the loaf.

8. Now bake until the top is golden brown, or for approximately 40 minutes or so.

9. Tent the bread with aluminum foil and bake until the top is firm and doesn't make a sound when pressed, or for another 30 to 45 minutes. Check if the internal temperatures have reached 200 degrees.

10. Let the bread cool then remove it from the pan and slice into 1/2 inch thick slices.

Calories 82, Carbs 3g, Protein 4g, Fat 7g

Macadamia Nut Bread

Yields 10 Slices

Ingredients

1/2 teaspoon apple cider vinegar

1/2 teaspoon baking soda

1/4 cup coconut flour

5 large eggs

5 oz. macadamia nuts

Directions

1. Begin by heating the oven to 350 degrees F.

2. Then add in macadamia nuts to a food processor or blender and pulse until you get nut butter. In case it proves hard to pulse without "a liquid", just add in eggs one at a time and pulse until you obtain nut-batter consistency.

3. Keep scrapping the sides of the food processor or blender and add in the rest of the eggs. Pulse until well blended.

4. Now add in baking soda, coconut flour and apple cider vinegar and then process until incorporated.

5. Get some grease and coat a medium sized loaf pan well. Add in the batter while smoothing the surface with a spatula.

Keto Bread

6. Put the pan in the bottom rack of the oven and bake until the top is golden brown, or for approximately 30 to 40 words.

7. Take out from the oven and let cool down while in the pan for about 15 or 20 minutes.

8. Then remove from the pan and store in an airtight container for 3 to 4 days at room temperature. You can also keep it refrigerated for up to 1 week.

Calories 151, Carbs 4g, Protein 5g, Fat 14g

Amazing Low Carb Keto Bread

Yields 10-12 slices

Ingredients

1/4 teaspoon sea salt

1 teaspoon baking powder

2 cups almond flour

1/2 cup melted ghee

7 large eggs

Directions

1. First heat your oven to 350 degrees F. Meanwhile, line a loaf pan with parchment so that it overlaps the sides.

2. Beat eggs in a large mixing bowl for a minute on high speed with a hand mixer. Add in meted ghee and continue beating until blended.

3. Lower the speed and slowly add the rest of the ingredients until fully blended and the batter becomes thick.

4. Move the batter to the parchment lined pan and smooth with a spatula. Now bake until the top is golden brown, or for about 40 to 45 minutes.

5. Cool the loaf on the rack for approximately 10 minutes and then slice. You can pile it high with sandwich toppings you like.

Calories, Carbs 3g, Protein 9g, Fat 24g

Coconut Flour Mini Cheese Loaves

Yields 18 Mini Loaves

Ingredients

100g grated/shredded cheese

1/2 finely sliced spring onion

8 medium eggs

1 teaspoon baking powder

50g coconut flour

113g butter softened

Pinch chilli, optional

Salt and pepper to taste

Coconut Flour Mini Cheese Loaves Toppings

2 tablespoon pumpkin seeds

1 pepperoni stick sliced

Directions

1. Combine the coconut flour with softened butter and add in chilli, pepper, salt and baking powder. Mix until smooth.

2. Add in eggs one by one while stirring at each addition. Stir the mixture through shredded or grated cheese and sliced spring onion. Reserve some cheese for topping the loaf.

3. Fill each mini loaf tin with the batter and top with pepperoni sticks if you like. Cover the contents with the cheese and sprinkle some pumpkin seeds if you like.

4. Now bake the loaf until golden brown, or for 15 minutes or so. Serve the loaf preferably warm with butter.

Calories 170, Carbs 2.8g, Protein 6.4g, Fat 13.8g

4-Ingredient Keto Almond Bread

Yields 12 Slices

Ingredients

2 cups almond flour

7 eggs

2 tablespoon coconut oil

½ cup butter

Directions

1. Heat your oven to 355 degrees F. Then get a parchment paper and line a loaf pan well.

2. In a bowl, add in eggs and mix on high speed for approximately 2 minutes.

3. Add in melted coconut oil, almond flour and the melted butter and mix until blended.

4. At this point, scrape the batter in to the prepared loaf pan

5. Bake the contents until a toothpick inserted into the bread comes out clean, or for about 45 to 50 minutes.

Calories: 178, Carbs 3.9g, Protein: 6.4g, Fat: 15g

Rosemary and Garlic Coconut Flour Bread

Yields 10 Slices

Ingredients

1/4 teaspoon pink himalayan salt

1/2 teaspoon onion powder

1/2 or 1 teaspoon garlic powder

2 teaspoon dried rosemary

1 teaspoon baking powder

6 large eggs

1/2 cup coconut flour

1 stick or 8 tablespoons butter

Directions

1. Mix together the dry ingredients (coconut flour, garlic, rosemary, onion, baking powder and salt) in a bowl. Set the mixture aside.

2. Add in the eggs to a another bowl and beat using a hand mixer until bubbles form at the top.

3. Melt the butter in a microwave and gradually add it to the eggs, beating with a hand mixer.

4. As soon as the dry ingredients and wet ones have blended in individual bowls, move the dry mixture into the wet ingredients mixing with a hand mixer.

5. Grease a 8 by 4 inch pan and pour the mixture. Spread it evenly in the pan.

6. Now bake the loaf in the oven at 350 degrees F until cooked through, or for 40 to 50 minutes.

7. Allow to cool for approximately 10 minutes and then remove from the pan. Slice it up and serve with butter.

Calories: 147, Carbs 3.5g, Protein: 4.6g, Fat: 12.5g

Zucchini Coconut Bread

Yields 10 Slices

Ingredients

1/2 teaspoon salt

1/2 cup erythritol

1/2 cup butter salted

6 large eggs

1 scoop unflavored protein powder

1 teaspoon vanilla extract

3/4 tablespoon baking powder

1/4 cup chopped pecan

1/2 cup grated zucchini, drained

3/4 cup coconut flour

Directions

1. Heat the oven to 350 degrees F. Then rinse the zucchini and shred it with a hand grater.

2. Add the zucchini to a bowl, season with salt and move it to a colander to drain extra fluid. Aim to get about 1/2 cup of shredded zucchini.

Keto Bread

3. Start preparing the dry mixture in a bowl. Just fold the coconut flour, protein powder, baking powder and the sweetener and mix the ingredients until well incorporated.

4. Now beat the eggs in a mixer along with melted butter and the vanilla extract.

5. Move the grated zucchini into the mixture and gradually add the dry ingredients mixture.

6. Whisk everything until well blended, and then drop the chopped pecan into the mixture.

7. Then coat a loaf pan with some butter and then spread it evenly into the prepared pan.

8. Put the loaf pan with the batter in the oven and bake until browned, or for about 40 to 45 minutes.

9. As soon as the surface of the bread is golden, remove from the oven and allow to cool down for about 10 minutes.

10. Then remove from the pan and slice it before serving.

Calories 160, Carbs: 1.7g, Protein: 6.9g, Fat: 14.3g

Double Chocolate Zucchini Bread

Yields 12 Slices

Ingredients

1/2 cup chocolate chips, sugar free

2 cups zucchini shredded

1 teaspoon vanilla

4 large eggs

1/4 cup melted or fractionated coconut oil

1/4 teaspoon salt

1 teaspoon baking powder

1 teaspoon baking soda

1/2 teaspoon ground cinnamon

1/2 cup Monk Fruit Granular Sweetener

1/2 cup cocoa powder, unsweetened

1/2 cup coconut flour

Directions

1. Mix together coconut flour, cinnamon, baking soda, cocoa, granular sweetener and salt in a large mixing bowl.

2. Blend in eggs, vanilla and coconut oil until incorporated.

3. Then fold the chocolate chips and zucchini and now pour the mixture onto parchment lined baking pan.

4. Bake the bread until a toothpick inserted in the center comes out clean, or for 45 to 55 minutes or so.

5. Once cooked through, remove from the oven and move to a cooling rack for about 15 minutes.

6. Remove from the pan and cool fully. Slice and enjoy.

Calories 124, Carbs 7g, Protein 4g, Fat 10g

Keto Collagen Protein Bread

Yields 10 Slices

Ingredients

1 tablespoon melted coconut oil

1 pinch sea salt

1 teaspoon baking powder keto friendly

1 teaspoon xanthan gum

3 tablespoons of coconut milk full-fat

6 tablespoons of coconut flour

5 egg whites and yolks separated

1/2 cup Perfect Keto Collagen

Directions

1. Heat your oven to 325 degrees F. Meanwhile, mix together all the dry ingredients in a bowl.

2. Now whisk together egg yolks, coconut milk and melted coconut oil in a small bowl and then set aside.

3. Whip the egg whites in a separate bowl until stiff peaks form.

4. At this point, fold the dry and the wet mixtures into the whipped egg and mix until blended.

5. Coat a loaf dish with some coconut oil and then pour the batter into the prepared dish.

6. Bake for approximately 40 minutes. Once cooked through, cool fully and set the bread.

Calories 98, Carbs 3g, Protein 7g, Fat 6g

Keto Bread

Yield 14 Slices

Ingredients

1 tablespoon poppy seeds

5 large eggs

1/2 cup filtered water

1/2 cup olive oil or avocado oil

1/2 teaspoon fine Himalayan salt

2 teaspoons baking powder

2 cups fine ground almond meal

Directions

1. Heat your oven to 400 degrees F. Then line a loaf pan with the parchment and set aside.

2. Mix together baking powder, almond meal and salt in a large bowl.

3. Meanwhile, drizzle in avocado oil until you obtain a crumbly dough. Make a small well in the dough and crack in the eggs.

4. Add in water and beat the eggs together while making small circles in the eggs until you obtain a light yellow and frothy mixture.

5. Now make bigger circles to hold the almond meal mix into it. Continue mixing in the same manner until you get a smooth, light and thick batter.

6. Pour the batter into a loaf pan and crape it out using a spatula. Sprinkle the contents with poppy seeds.

7. Bake in the center rack of the preheated oven for approximately 40 minutes or until its hard and golden brown.

8. At this point, remove from the oven and allow to sit for about 30 minutes.

9. Unmold and slice the loaf. Alternatively, store the bread in an airtight container for not more than 5 days. Just toast to heat up and serve!

Calories: 227, Carbs 4g, Protein: 7g, Fat: 21g

Lemon Blueberry Zucchini Bread

Yields 6 Slices

Ingredients

1 cup blueberries

1 1/2 cups grated zucchini

1/4 teaspoon sea salt

2 teaspoons gluten-free baking powder

2 cups blanched almond flour

1 teaspoon vanilla extract

1 tablespoon lemon zest, optional

1 tablespoon lemon juice

3 large eggs

3/4 cup erythritol

1/2 cup butter (softened)

Lemon Glaze

4 teaspoons of lemon juice

1/4 cup Erythritol

Directions

Keto Bread

1. First grate the zucchini and then drain over the sink.

2. Heat the oven to 325 degrees F and then line a 9 by 5 loaf pan with parchment or well-greased foil.

3. Beat together erythritol and butter in a large bowl until fluffy.

4. Also beat in eggs, lemon zest, lemon juice and vanilla extract. Beat in almond flour, sea salt and baking powder.

5. Wrap the zucchini in sturdy paper towels layers or a cheesecloth and squeeze it over the sink to remove any available liquid.

6. Then stir the drained zucchini into a bowl and mix well. Now fold the berries on to the egg and flour mixture.

7. Move the batter the parchment lined pan and smooth it while rounding the top evenly using a spoon.

8. Bake the loaf until an inserted toothpick comes out clean, or for approximately 60 to 70 minutes.

9. Cool the bread fully in the pan and start making the glaze. Just run the sweetener though the blender to ground it and then whisk it along with lemon juice.

10. To serve, drizzle the lemon juice and powdered sweetener glaze over the loaf.

Calories 139, Carbs 5g, Fat 12g, Protein 4g

Keto Bread Low-Carb

Yields 20 Slices

Ingredients:

2 tablespoons coconut flour

3 teaspoons apple cider vinegar

¾ teaspoon baking soda

3–4 tablespoons butter, melted

¼ teaspoon cream of tartar

6 egg whites

1½ cups almond flour

Directions

1. First preheat your oven to 375 degrees F.

2. To the egg white, add cream of tartar and then whip the eggs using a hand mixer until soft peaks are well formed.

3. At this point, add baking soda, butter, almond flour, coconut flour and apple cider vinegar to a food processor. Process until well blended.

4. Put the mixture in a bowl and now fold into the egg mixture. Grease an 8 by 4 loaf pan and then pour in the entire mixture.

Keto Bread

5. Bake until cooked through, or for around 30 minutes.

Calories 65, Carbs 2.4g, Protein 3.1g, Fat 6g

The Best Keto Bread

Yields 10 Slices

Ingredients

3 egg whites

1 cup boiling water

2 teaspoons apple cider vinegar

1 teaspoon salt

2 teaspoons baking powder

5 tablespoons ground flax seeds or psyllium husk powder

1 1/4 cups almond flour

2 tablespoons sesame seeds, optional

Directions

1. Heat your oven to 350 degrees F. Meanwhile, butter and line a loaf pan (9 by 5 inch capacity) with parchment paper. Set the loaf tin aside.

2. Mix together almond flour, salt, baking powder and psyllium husk until blended.

3. Add in apple cider vinegar and egg whites and then beat with an electric mixer on medium speed until you obtain dough with paste consistency.

4. Set the speed to low and then steam in 1 cup of boiling water. Then set the speed to high and mix until you get an elastic play-dough consistency, or for another 30 seconds.

5. Move the dough on the parchment-lined baking tin and smooth the top with a spoon.

6. Sprinkle a little sesame seeds and then bake until the top rises and puffs up, or for about 55 to 65 minutes.

7. At this point, remove from the oven and let cool, and then move the bread to a cooling rack.

8. Slice and serve. You can store any leftovers at room temperature for 2 days, covered. You can then move to the fridge for not more than another 2 days.

Calories 53, Carbs 4g, Protein 2g, Fat 3g

Flat Bread

Keto Flatbread

Serves 6

Ingredients

1/8 teaspoon garlic powder

1/4 cup spinach cooked and drained

2 tablespoons almond flour

1 egg

1 tablespoon cream cheese

3/4 cup shredded low moisture mozzarella cheese

Salt to taste

Directions

1. Preheat your oven to 350 degrees F.

2. Meanwhile, in a heat safe bowl, melt cream cheese and mozzarella cheese in the microwave in 30 seconds intervals. Mix to combine in between the 30 seconds bursts.

3. As soon as the cheese has melted and is fully combined, mix in almond flour, egg and the cooked spinach.

4. Flatten the cheese and egg mixture on a parchment lined baking sheet, and season with some salt and garlic cloves.

5. Bake for approximately 15 minutes, and then flip. Bake the second side until crisp, or for another 5 minutes or so.

Calories 75, Carbs 1g, Protein 5g, Fat 5g

Easy Flatbread

Serves 1

Ingredients

1 teaspoon coconut flour

1 tablespoon olive oil

1 ½ tablespoons cream cheese

1 large egg

¾ cup mozzarella cheese, part skim, shredded

Optional:

0.1g xanthan gum

Garlic powder

Dried Italian herbs

Pepper

Salt

Keto Bread

Directions

1. Preheat your oven to 350 degrees F. Meanwhile line your baking sheet with parchment.

2. Mix the cream cheese and egg at room temperature and then stir well with a fork.

3. Add in the rest of the ingredients and stir to incorporate.

4. Spread the mixture on the lined baking sheet into an 8-inch circle.

5. Bake the flatbread in the center of your oven for approximately 30 minutes.

6. Flip the flatbread halfway through cooking time to cook the other side too.

Carbs 4g, Protein 27g, Fat 39g

3-Ingredient Flatbread

Serves: 4

Ingredients

½ cup almond flour

½ teaspoon baking powder

8 egg whites

Optional 1 teaspoon each:

Coconut oil

Organic coconut palm sugar

Thyme

Red pepper flakes

Basil

Rosemary

Garlic powder

Salt

Directions

1. Lightly whisk the egg whites in a medium bowl.

2. Add in salt, baking powder, almond flour and the spices if you like. Whisk until the mixture is lump free.

3. Coat a cooking pan with a little coconut oil. Scoop approximately ½ cup of the batter onto the sprayed pan.

4. Cover the batter with a lid and then cook until the bread is airy and bubbly, or for about 2 minutes or so.

5. Remove the lid from the pan and flip the flatbread. Cool for an additional 1 minute or so.

Calories 102, Carbs 3g, Protein 4g, Fat 6g

Rosemary Garlic Flatbread

Serves 4

Ingredients

2 cloves garlic crushed

1/2 teaspoon rosemary

2 tablespoons butter

2 tablespoons coconut flour

1 egg beaten

1 tablespoon cream cheese

1 cup mozzarella

Directions

1. Preheat your oven to 400 degrees F.

2. Into a heat safe bowl, add in cream cheese and mozzarella and cook in the microwave for approximately 1 minute.

3. Stir the cheeses well until they are melted, and then add in egg and coconut flour.

4. Coat a cookie sheet with oil and spread it with your hands.

5. Combine butter, rosemary and garlic and brush the mixture over the dough.

6. Bake the dough until golden brown, or for about 15 minutes. Allow to cool and then enjoy!

Calories 217, Carbs 6g, Protein 5.5g, Fat 12.8g

Coconut Flour Flatbread

Serves 6

Ingredients

1 teaspoon salt

1 cup canned coconut milk, full fat

¼ cup coconut flour

½ cup arrowroot flour or tapioca flour

Directions

1. Over medium heat, pre-heat a steel crepe pan or a 9.5-inch non-stick cooking pan.

2. Mix everything in a bowl, and once incorporated, pour ¼ cup of the mixture into the cooking pan.

3. Spread the batter throughout the pan using a spoon. Cook until mostly cooked and firm in appearance, or for approximately 2 to 3 minutes and then flip.

4. Cook the other side for another 2 minutes or until well cooked.

5. Serve or cool on a wire rack until ready to serve.

Calories 128, Carbs 12.7g, Protein 1.8g, Fat 8.5g

Low Carb Flatbread

Serves: 6

Ingredients

1 cup rapidly boiling water

3 tablespoons salted butter, melted

1/4 teaspoon Italian seasoning, optional

1 teaspoon baking powder

1/4 teaspoon salt

2 tablespoons psyllium husk powder

1/2 cup coconut flour

Directions

1. In a bowl, whisk the dry ingredients until well incorporated.

2. Add in the melted butter and mix until blended. Pour in the hot water to the mixture.

3. Divide the dough onto equally sized balls. Then roll individual balls between two parchment papers. Make the balls 1/16 inch thick.

4. Discard the parchment and dry fry the balls for 2 to 3 minutes per side in cast iron skillet on medium high heat.

Keto Bread

5. Serve hot.

Calories: 104, Carbs: 8g, Protein: 1g, Fat: 7g

Low Carb Indian Flatbread

Serves 2

Ingredients

1/2 cup boiling water

1 teaspoon beef gelatin in 1 tablespoon boiling water

1 1/2 tablespoons coconut oil or ghee

1/8 teaspoon salt

1/8 teaspoon baking powder

1/2 tablespoon psyllium husk powder

3 tablespoons coconut flour

Directions

1. In a medium bowl, whisk together coconut flour, baking powder, psyllium husk powder and salt until incorporated.

2. Add in ghee, boiling water and dissolved gelatin, and mix until you get firm dough.

3. Divide the dough into two balls and flatten them in between plastic wrap or parchment paper into 5 inch circle.

4. Over medium-high heat, preheat a non-stick skillet and then add in some ghee. Heat until melted and then add a dough circle. Lower the heat to medium, and cook the

flathead for approximately 12 minutes or until golden on both sides; while flipping as required.

5. Repeat for the other flatbreads and then serve warm.

Calories 190, Carbs 8g, Protein 3g, Fat 16g

Buns/Rolls

Fluffy Keto Buns

Serves 4

Ingredients

1 teaspoon baking powder

1 tablespoons psyllium husk powder

1/4 cup coconut flour

1/4 cup almond flour

1/4 cup boiling hot water

1 egg, room temperature

3 egg whites, room temperature

Sesame seeds, optional

Directions

1. Preheat your oven to 350 degrees F.

2. Meanwhile mix all the dry ingredients until well incorporated.

3. Add everything to a food processor or electric blender and mix for about 20 seconds or until smooth.

4. Allow the dough to rest for a few minutes to absorb moisture.

5. Separate it into equal portions and make about 4 buns.

6. Put the buns on a parchment paper-lined baking sheet. Top with seeds you like such as sesame seeds or others.

7. Make a criss-cross cutting on top of the dough and bake until browned, or for approximately 25 minutes.

Calories 109, Carbs 8.3g, Protein 7.3g, Fat 5.5g

Best Keto Dinner Rolls

Serves 6

Ingredients

1/2 teaspoon baking soda

1 egg

1/4 cup ground flax seed

1 cup almond flour

1 ounce cream cheese

1 cup mozzarella, shredded

Directions

1. Preheat the oven to 400 degrees F. Meanwhile get a parchment paper and line the baking sheet. Set aside.

2. Mix mozzarella cheese and cream cheese in a medium bowl, and microwave for about 1 minute.

3. Stir the cheeses until combined, and add in the egg. Stir to incorporate.

4. Mix together baking soda, flax seeds and almond flour in a separate bowl.

5. Combine the egg and the cheese mixture and stir together to have soft-ball looking dough.

Keto Bread

6. Wet your hand and roll the ball into 6 balls. Roll the balls into the sesame seeds if you like, and then put them onto a baking sheet.

7. Bake until brown, or for approximately 10 to 12 minutes. Let them cool for another 15 minutes then serve.

Calories: 219, Carbs: 5.6g, Protein 10g, Fat: 18g

Keto Burger Buns

Serves: 6

Ingredients

4 tablespoons butter, melted

1 teaspoon kosher salt

2 teaspoons baking powder

3 cups almond flour

3 large eggs

4 ounces cream cheese

2 cups shredded mozzarella

Dried parsley

Sesame seeds

Directions

1. Preheat the oven to 400 degrees F. Meanwhile line a baking sheet with parchment.

2. Melt the cream cheese and the mozzarella in a large heat-safe bowl until combined.

3. Add in the eggs and stir to mix. Add in salt, baking powder and almond flour, and mix once more.

4. Make 6 balls from the resulting dough, and then slightly flatten them. Put the balls on the lined baking sheet.

5. Brush the balls with butter and sprinkle with parsley and sesame seeds.

6. Bake them for about 10 to 12 minutes, or until golden. Serve and enjoy!

Calories: 156, Carbs 1.8g, Protein 5.6g, Fat 14.5g

Keto Hamburger Buns

Serves: 4

Ingredients

1 teaspoon sesame seeds

3 large eggs

1 ounce butter melted

2 tablespoons warm water

1 teaspoon inulin

1 teaspoon yeast dried

1/2 teaspoon xanthan gum

1/2 teaspoon baking powder

2 teaspoons psyllium husk powder

1 cup almond flour

Directions

1. Combine the xanthan gum, baking powder, psyllium husk powder and almond flour in a mixing bowl until well blended.

2. Form a well in the center of the mixture and add in inulin, yeast and warm water. Mix the ingredients and let this sit until the yeast is foamy, or for about 5 minutes.

3. Add in eggs, butter and mix well. Meanwhile get some olive oil and grease your muffin top pan.

4. Spoon the batter between 4 holes and sprinkle some sesame seeds.

5. Let this sit for approximately 15 minutes. Meanwhile preheat the oven to 340 degrees F.

6. Bake the buns until they are golden brown and can spring back when touched, or for approximately 15 to 20 minutes.

7. Let them cool on a wire rack and then serve.

Calories: 278, Carbs: 9g, Protein: 12g, Fat: 21g

Cheesy Keto Hamburger Buns

Serves 6 buns

Ingredients

4 tablespoon grass-fed butter, melted

3 cups almond flour

4 large eggs

4 ounces cream cheese

2 cups shredded mozzarella cheese

Sesame seeds

Directions

1. Preheat your oven to 400 degrees F. Get parchment paper and line your baking sheet, and then set aside.

2. Mix the cream cheese and mozzarella in a large bowl and then add in 3 eggs.

3. Stir to blend and then add in almond flour.

4. Make 6 buns from the dough and then set them on the parchment lined baking sheet.

5. Brush the buns with some butter and the remaining egg. Sprinkle with some sesame seeds and place in the oven.

Keto Bread

6. Bake the buns for approximately 10 to 12 minutes, or until golden.

Calories 287, Carbs 2.4g, Protein 14.7g, Fat 25.8g

Best Keto bread rolls

Serves 8

Ingredients

2 tablespoons sesame seeds

2 teaspoons white vinegar

3 egg whites

1 cup boiling water

1 teaspoon sea salt

5 tablespoons psyllium husk

1 1/2 cups blanched almond flour

Cooking spray

Directions

1. Preheat your oven to 350 degrees F. Using cooking spray, grease a baking sheet and then set aside.

2. Mix the psyllium husk, almond flour and salt in a bowl until combined.

3. Add in vinegar, egg whites, water and then use an electric mixer to whisk the mixture for about 1 minute or until well incorporated.

4. As soon as you get thick dough, wet your hands and shape into about 8 rolls.

5. Arrange them on the greased baking sheet and then top with the sesame seeds.

6. Bake the bread rolls for approximately 55 minutes, or until golden.

Calories 166, Carbs 9.6g, Protein 6.8g, Fat 12.9g

Almond Flour Goji Buns

Serves 10

Ingredients

1 tablespoon stevia powder, sweetener

2 tablespoons cooking cream

Pinch of salt

1 teaspoon baking powder

1 tablespoon flax seed, ground

2 tablespoons goji berries, dried and ground

3 tablespoons almond flour, preferably Bob's Red Mill

5 tablespoons coconut oil

4 eggs

30g salted butter

Directions

1. Preheat your oven to 350 degrees F.

2. Using an electric mixer, beat eggs well in a medium sized or large bowl.

3. Mix in the oil into the eggs, gradually adding a tablespoon at each addition and continue to whisk.

4. Once done, mix in the cream into the mixture, adding a tablespoon at a time and whisking until fully incorporated.

5. Add in some warm melted butter into the mixture, and combine with the rest of the ingredients fully, before adding the liquid sweetener.

6. Add in the dry ingredients comprising of salt, baking powder, flax seed, goji beans and almond flour to the cream batter. You just need to add a tablespoon at each time, as you gently mix by hand.

7. Once done, transfer the dough to a non-stick cup bun tray.

8. Bake the cups in the hot oven for around 15 minutes, up until the buns top are golden. After removing the baked buns from the oven, they will deflate slightly.

9. At this point serve while hot, and then store the remaining cups in the fridge if you like.

Nutritional information per serving: Calories 145, Carbs 2.6g, Proteins 3.2g, Fat 13.6g

Waffles

Keto Waffles Stuffed with Cream Cheese

Serves 4

Ingredients

2 tablespoons cream cheese

1 tablespoon almond flour

4 tablespoons mayonnaise

4 eggs large

1 teaspoon cooking oil

Directions

1. Grease your waffle iron with some cooking oil and then preheat the iron.

2. Mix the almond flour, mayonnaise and eggs in the blender or using a hand mixer until you have a smooth mixture.

3. Cut the cream cheese into 1cm cubes, and add the batter to the preheated waffle iron.

4. Distribute ¼ of the cream cheese cubes throughout the waffle wells before you cover with a lid.

5. Close the lid and cook until the waffles are golden brown, or for about 3 to 5 minutes.

Keto Bread

Calories 201, Carbs 1g, Protein 6g, Fat 19g

Vanilla Keto Waffles

Serves: 5

Ingredients

125g butter melted

3 tablespoons full fat milk or cream

2 teaspoons vanilla

1 teaspoon baking powder

4 tablespoons granulated sweetener

4 tablespoons coconut flour

5 medium eggs, separated

Directions

1. Whisk the egg whites in a bowl thoroughly until you have firm and stiff peaks.

2. In a separate bowl, combine coconut flour, egg yolks, baking powder and the granulated sweetener until blended.

3. Gradually add in melted butter, and continue mixing until you have a smooth batter.

4. Add in vanilla and the full fat milk, and mix well.

5. Fold spoonfuls of the whisked egg whites into the egg yolks and try to maintain as much of air puffiness as you can.

6. Put sufficient amount of the waffle mixture into a preheated waffle maker.

7. Cook one waffle until it is golden and repeat with the rest of the batter until you are done.

Calories 280, Carbs 4.5g, Protein 7g, Fat 26g

Low Carb Waffles

Serves: 1

Ingredients

1/2 teaspoon baking powder

1 tablespoon coconut oil or melted butter

2 – 4 tablespoons almond flour

2 ounces cream cheese

2 large eggs

Directions

1. Put everything in a blender and process until smooth.

2. Pour the batter in a hot and greased waffle maker and cook the waffle for approximately 2 to 3 minutes or based on the waffle maker's directions.

3. Once ready to serve, lift the waffle off the grid with a fork and enjoy!

Calories 522, Carbs 7g, Protein 19g, Fat 48g

Keto Waffles with Blueberry Butter

Serves 4

Ingredients

1ounce. fresh blueberries

3ounce. butter

Blueberry Butter

1/3 cup coconut flour

2 teaspoons baking powder

1 teaspoon vanilla extract

8 eggs

5ounce. melted butter

Directions

1. Mix the eggs and melted butter and then add in the rest of the ingredients.

2. Mix until you obtain a smooth batter and then let it rest for approximately 5 minutes.

3. Preheat a waffle iron to medium.

4. Pour the batter into the hot waffle iron and cook approximately until golden. Repeat until all batter is used.

5. Mix together blueberries and butter using an electric mixture. Serve the waffles with the berry butter.

Calories 575, Carbs 8g, Protein 14g, Fat 56g

Protein Waffles

Serves: 1

Ingredients

1 teaspoon baking powder

3 tablespoons sour cream

1 egg

1/2 cup whey protein powder

Pinch of salt

Directions

1. Heat waffle iron on medium heat setting and then coat it well with cooking spray.

2. Mix baking powder, sour cream, egg, protein powder and salt in a medium bowl.

3. Once fully combined, pour half of the mixture (or less) into the hot waffle iron and cook based on waffle maker instructions.

4. Serve the waffle with butter and enjoy!

Calories 252

Low Carb Waffles

Serves: 8

Ingredients

3 teaspoons baking powder

1/2 cup coconut flour

2 tablespoon powdered Stevia

8 eggs

8 ounces cream cheese

Directions

1. Add everything into a blender and then puree on high speed for about 1 minute or until smooth.

2. Meanwhile heat a waffle iron. Then spray to with non-stick spray.

3. Add approximately 1/8th of the batter into the hot waffle iron and cook until golden.

4. Repeat until all batter is used. Add some almond milk if you find the batter too thick.

Calories 193, Carbs 6g, Protein 8g, Fat 14g

Bread Sticks

Bread Sticks With Mozzarella Dough

Serves: 20

Ingredients

1 medium egg

Pinch salt

2 tablespoons cream cheese

85g almond meal/flour

170g grated or pre-shredded mozzarella cheese

Optional Flavors

1 tablespoons parsley fresh or dried

1 teaspoon dried rosemary

1 tablespoon garlic crushed

Directions

1. Put almond flour, cream cheese, salt and shredded mozzarella in a heat safe bowl.

2. Season with your preferred flavors and then put in the microwave for approximately 1 minute.

Keto Bread

3. Stir and then set heat to HIGH, and microwave for another 30 seconds.

4. Add in the medium-sized egg and mix until you have a cheesy dough.

5. Cut a small part of the dough and roll into a long but thin bread stick. Repeat for the rest of the dough.

4. Put the breadsticks in a sheet pan or parchment lined baking tray.

5. Bake at 425 degrees F until they are golden brown, or for approximately 10 minutes.

Calories 58, Carbs 1.2g, Protein 3.1g, Fat 4.9g

Keto Cheesy Breadsticks

Serves 10

Ingredients

Breadsticks

¼ teaspoon salt

¼ teaspoon baking soda

½ teaspoon garlic powder

½ teaspoon cream of tartar

1 ½ teaspoons Italian seasoning

¼ cup + 1 tablespoon coconut flour

1 ounce cream cheese, softened

¼ cup (2 ounces) softened unsalted butter

¼ cup + 1 tablespoon Parmesan cheese, grated

1 ¼ cups shredded mozzarella cheese

4 eggs

Topping:

½ teaspoon Italian seasoning

¼ cup grated Parmesan cheese

2 cups shredded mozzarella cheese

Directions

1. Preheat your oven to 350 degrees F. Get some cooking spray and coat an 8 by 8 baking pan.

2. Using an electric mixer, mix cream cheese, butter, grated Parmesan and shredded mozzarella cheeses along with eggs in a mixing bowl.

3. Once well combined, add in baking soda, garlic, cream of tartar, salt, Italian seasoning and coconut flour. Transfer the mixture to the coated baking pan.

4. To make the topping, combine all the ingredients for "topping" in a separate mixing bowl.

5. Once fully incorporated, sprinkle the topping on your breadsticks. Put the pan in the oven and bake in the middle rack for approximately 40 minutes.

6. Remove from the oven and broil the breadsticks for about 1 to 2 minutes, or until brown and bubbly.

7. Remove the breadsticks from the pan and let them cool. Cut into bite-size pieces and enjoy.

Calories 213, Carbs 4.6g, Protein 13g, Fat 15.9g

Cheesy Garlic Breadsticks

Serves: 2

Ingredients

1 teaspoon garlic powder

1 egg

1 cup grated Parmesan cheese

1 cup mozzarella, shredded

Directions

1. Begin by preheating your oven to 350 degrees F. Using a parchment paper, line a baking sheet well and set aside.

2. Mix everything in a bowl, until fully blended. Put the mixture on the lined baking sheet and flatten it like a pizza crust.

3. Bake for approximately 15 minutes, and then set your oven to "broil". Move the breadsticks to the top rack of the oven and broil until brown.

4. Slice the breadsticks using a pizza cutter and serve. You can dip them in sugar-free marinara sauce and garnish with parsley flakes, red pepper and Italian seasoning.

Calories 130, Carbs 7.0g, Protein 11g, Fat 17g

Keto Breadstick Twists

Serves 10

Ingredients

½ cup almond flour

4 tablespoons coconut flour

½ teaspoon salt

1 teaspoon baking powder

6 ½ ounces cups shredded mozzarella cheese

2 ounces butter

1 egg

2 ounces green pesto

1 egg

Directions

1. Preheat your oven to 350 degrees F. Mix all the dry ingredients in a bowl.

2. In a pot, melt the butter and cheese on low heat. Stir the mixture using a wooden fork until you obtain smooth batter.

3. Crack in the egg and blend well. Add in the dry ingredients and combine to get firm dough.

4. Put the dough between two parchment papers and roll using a rolling pin to form a rectangle that is 1/5 inch thick.

5. Discard the upper piece of parchment and then spread pesto on the dough.

6. Cut the dough into 1 inch strips and then twist the breadsticks and place on a parchment paper lined baking sheet.

7. Bake until golden brown, or for about 15 to 20 minutes.

Calories 194, Carbs 1g, Protein: 17g, Fat: 17g

Cauliflower Breadsticks

Serves 4

Ingredients

2 eggs

1 cup mozzarella or Mexican blend cheese, shredded

1/2 teaspoon Salt

1 teaspoon Italian Seasoning

1/2 teaspoon ground pepper

1/2 teaspoon granulated garlic

2 cups riced cauliflower

For Topping

1/4 cup Parmesan cheese, grated

Directions

1. Line a 9 by 13 baking sheet with parchment paper or alternatively, spray it with butter or vegetable oil and then set aside.

2. Preheat the oven to 350 degrees F, and put the eggs at the bottom part of a food processor or a large blender.

3. Add in shredded cheese, salt, Italian seasoning, pepper, garlic, cheese and riced cauliflower.

Keto Bread

4. Process or blend on low speed until the cauliflower is broken down fully and the mixture is well blended.

5. Transfer the cauliflower mixture on the pan and then pat the dough to make an even layer that is ¼ inch thick.

6. Bake the dough for approximately 30 minutes and then remove from the oven.

7. Sprinkle the dough on top with grated cheese and broil on high setting until the cheese is melted and brown, or for about 2 to 3 minutes.

8. Remove the dough from the broiler and slice it into breadsticks.

Calories 165, Carbs 5g, Fat 10g, Protein 13g

Low Carb Cheesy Breadsticks

Serves: 8

Ingredients

For the Breadsticks:

1/2 cup shredded Parmesan cheese

1⅓ cup shredded mozzarella cheese

1/2 teaspoon garlic powder

1 teaspoon Italian seasoning

¼ teaspoon baking powder

¼ teaspoon salt

4 eggs

1 ounce softened cream cheese

⅓ cup coconut flour

4½ tablespoons of melted & cooled butter

For the Top:

1/2 teaspoon Italia shredded cheese

2 cups mozzarella shredded cheese

1/2 teaspoon Italian seasoning

Keto Bread

Directions

1. Preheat your oven to 400 degrees F. Meanwhile grease a 1 by 7 baking sheet and set aside.

2. Mix cream cheese, salt, eggs and butter and then whisk until blended.

3. Add in coconut flour, spices and baking powder; stir to incorporate.

4. Stir in the shredded cheeses and pour the batter into a casserole dish.

5. Top the batter with more Parmesan and mozzarella cheese and your preferred spices.

6. Bake the breadsticks until cooked through, or for about 15 minutes.

7. Halfway through the baking, get a pizza cutter and then cut horizontally down the middle,

8. Cut the dough vertically approximately after every 1 inch to get individual breadsticks.

9. Transfer the cooking pan to the top of the oven and broil until the cheese is brown and bubbly, or for about 1 to 2 minutes.

10. Serve the breadsticks with no sugar marinara sauce.

Calories: 299, Carbs 4g, Protein 17g, Fat 23g

Low Carb Cauliflower Breadsticks

Serves 5

Ingredients

3/4 cup shredded mozzarella cheese

1/2 teaspoon ground black pepper

1 teaspoon salt

1/2 tablespoons chopped fresh Italian flat-leaf parsley

1/2 tablespoon chopped fresh basil

1/2 tablespoon garlic minced

1 large egg

1/2 cup shaved parmesan cheese

1/2 cup shredded mozzarella cheese

1 head raw cauliflower

Directions

1. Preheat the oven to 425 degrees F. Line a baking sheet using a parchment paper or alternatively use a silicone baking mat.

2. Core and break the cauliflower into florets and put in the bowl of a food processor. Pulse the florets to achieve rice consistency.

3. Now mix the riced cauliflower and all the ingredients apart from ¾ cup shredded mozzarella cheese and 1/2 cup shaved Parmesan cheese in a large bowl.

4. Once mixed well, put the batter onto a parchment-lined baking sheet and then spread to make a rectangle shape of about 9x7 inch, and ¼ inch thick.

5. Bake the dough in the oven for 10 to 12 minutes, then remove from the oven and top with the reserved mozzarella cheese.

6. Return to the oven and bake until the cheese melts and begins to brown. Cool for around 10 minutes then cut it into breadsticks.

7. Garnish the cauliflower breadsticks with Parmesan cheese. Serve with red sauce of your choice.

Calories 143, Carbs 2g, Protein 11g, Fat 9g

Crackers

Seed Crackers

Serves 30

Ingredients

1 cup boiling water

¼ cup melted coconut oil

1 teaspoon salt

1 tablespoon ground psyllium husk powder

⅓ cup sesame seeds

⅓ cup flax seed or chia seeds

⅓ cup pumpkin seeds

⅓ cup sunflower seeds

⅓ cup almond flour

Directions

1. Preheat your oven to 300 degrees F. Meanwhile mix all the dry ingredients in a bowl.

2. Add in coconut oil and boiling water and then mix using a wooden fork.

3. Continue working on the dough until you obtain a ball that has gel-like appearance.

4. Put the dough on a parchment paper lined baking sheet and cover with another parchment.

5. Using a rolling pin, gently flatten the dough evenly and then discard the top parchment.

6. Bake the dough on the lower rack of your oven for approximately 45 minutes, while checking on it now and again. Keep an eye on the seeds.

7. Once ready, remove from the oven and let the crackers dry inside the oven.

8. Break the cool crackers and top them with butter before serving.

Calories 61, Carbs 2g, Protein 2g, Fat 6g

Almond Flour Crackers

Serves 6

Ingredients

1 large beaten egg

1/2 teaspoon Sea salt

2 cups blanched almond flour

Directions

1. Preheat the oven to 350 degrees F. Line your baking sheet with parchment.

2. In a large bowl combine the almond flour and salt and then add in the egg. Mix until you get firm dough. Alternatively do the mixing in a food processor.

3. Position the dough in between two parchment papers and then roll with a rolling pin into a rectangle that's about 2/16 inch thick.

4. Cut the dough into rectangles and then prick with a toothpick or fork if necessary.

5. Put the dough on the prepared baking sheet and bake until its golden, or for about 8 to 12 minutes.

Nutritional information per serving: Calories 226, Carbs 8g, Protein 9g, Fat 19g

Spicy Ranch Crackers

Serves 4

Ingredients

1/2 teaspoon red pepper flakes

1 tablespoon ranch seasoning mix

1 large egg

3/4 cup almond flour

2 tablespoons cream cheese

2 cups grated mozzarella

Directions

1. Begin by preheating the oven to 425 degrees F.

2. Into a heat safe bowl, add in cream cheese and mozzarella and microwave the cheeses at 30 seconds bursts until fully melted.

3. Stir the cheese mixture and then add in the egg, almond flour, red pepper flaked and ranch seasoning.

4. Put the dough on a parchment paper and cover with another sheet of paper. Roll the dough to about ¼ inch in thickness.

5. Using a pizza cutter or sharp knife, cut the dough into squares measuring 1 inch or so to get about 60 pieces.

6. Move the crackers to the prepared baking sheet and place in the oven. Bake them for about 5 minutes, flip over and bake for another 5 minutes.

7. Allow to cool and then serve

Nutritional information per serving: Calories 235, Carbs 4g, Protein 17g, Fat 18g

Cheese Thyme Keto Crackers

Serves 8

Ingredients

1 egg

1/4 cup parmesan, grated

1/2 cup strong cheddar, grated

2 tablespoons melted butter

3 tablespoons coconut flour

Thyme leaves

Directions

1. Preheat the oven to 180 degrees C. Meanwhile combine parmesan, ¼ cup of grated cheddar, egg, melted butter and coconut flour until well blended.

2. Allow the mixture to rest for a couple of minutes for the flour to absorb the liquids.

3. Make 8 balls and put them on a parchment lined baking sheet.

4. Press the dough with your hand to form small flat disks and then top with the ¼ cup of cheddar on top.

5. Season with dried thyme or thyme leaves and bake until the edges are well browned, or for about 12 to 15 minutes.

Calories 60, Carbs 0.7g, Fat 5.1g, Protein 0g

Grain-Free Crackers

Serves 6

Ingredients

1/2 teaspoon sea salt

3 egg whites

2 sun dried tomatoes

1 teaspoon garlic powder

1 teaspoon crushed red pepper flakes

1 cup walnuts

1/4 cup flax seeds

1 cup raw almonds

Directions

1. Preheat your oven to 300 degrees F.

2. Add all ingredients in a blender or food processor and pulse until you have dough.

3. Place a parchment paper on a baking sheet and spread the mixture on the paper, very thinly.

4. Bake the crackers for about 1 hour, and then remove from the oven to cool.

5. Once cooled, break into pieces and store the crackers.

Nutritional information per serving; Calories 143, Carbs 5.6g, Protein 5.9g, Fat 12.0g

Mustard Crackers

Serves 15

Ingredients

2 1/2 tablespoons coconut flour

1 tablespoon wholegrain mustard

Pinch of salt

2 tablespoons sesame seeds

1 egg

1 tablespoon melted or coconut oil, butter or ghee

3 tablespoons tahini paste

Directions

1. Preheat your oven to 338 degrees F.

2. In a bowl, combine mustard, salt, sesame seeds, egg, butter and tahini.

3. Into this mixture, add coconut flour and then combine until it thickens. In case you are not using coconut floor, add more flour since coconut is a moisture absorber.

4. Start rolling the mixture into a ball and then position the ball on a baking paper or parchment paper that is slightly greased. It should measure around 40cm by 40cm.

5. Using your hands flatten it in the middle until you form a flat pancake; and then use a different parchment paper to cover.

6. Now flatten the pan cake using a rolling pin until you make a 3-5mm thin layer. Start from the middle and roll the dough evenly into 4 directions.

7. At this point, make a small incision mark using a knife. Cut both vertically and horizontally to help the cracker break easily after cooking.

8. Position the contents on the middle shelf of your oven and then cook for around 15 minutes.

9. Once the outer edges appear cooked, remove from heat and slice the edges off. Cook for an additional 3-5 minutes, or until cooked through.

10. Put the cooked cracker layer to cool. Serve and enjoy.

Nutritional information per serving; Calories 43, Carbs 1.1g, Protein 1.4g, Fat 4.4g

Pizza Crust

Almond Flour Pizza Crust

Serves 8

Ingredients

1 tablespoon olive oil

2 tablespoons water

2 large eggs

1/2 teaspoon garlic powder

1/2 teaspoon basil

1/2 teaspoon oregano

1/2 teaspoon baking powder

1 tablespoon whole psyllium husks or flax meal

1/2 cup grated Parmesan cheese

1 1/2 cups almond flour

Directions

1. Mix almond flour, garlic powder, basil, oregano, baking powder, whole psyllium husks and Parmesan cheese in a large bowl.

2. Mix the eggs, olive oil and water in another small bowl.

3. Pour in the olive oil and egg mixture into the dry ingredients and stir until you have firm dough. If need be add some more water.

4. Make a ball from the dough and then roll it between two parchment papers. Transfer the rolled dough into a pizza pan and discard the top parchment.

5. Bake the pizza crust at 373 degrees F until the crust is browned, or for approximately 20 to 25 minutes.

5. Let the crust cool for another 10 to 15 minutes, and then flip over the crust pizza and discard the second parchment paper.

6. Season with pizza sauce and your preferred toppings. Put it under the broiler and broil until cooked though.

7. Alternatively, you can bake at 425 degrees F for another 5 to 10 minutes or so. Serve and enjoy.

Nutritional information per serving: Calories 182, Carbs 6g, Protein 8g, Fat 14g

Parmesan & Almond Flour Pizza Crust

Serves 8

Ingredients

1/2 teaspoon garlic powder

1/4 teaspoon crushed red pepper flakes

3/4 teaspoon basil

3/4 teaspoon oregano

1/2 teaspoon xylitol

1/2 teaspoon baking powder

1/2 cup grated Parmesan cheese

1 1/2 cups blanched almond flour

1 tablespoon extra-virgin olive oil

1/4 cup tap water

1 large egg

Directions

1. Begin by whisking water, egg and oil in a small bowl. Set the mixture aside.

2. Mix the rest of the ingredients. Add in the egg and oil mixture and mix to form a thick dough.

3. Grease two parchment papers and roll the dough in between them to form a square or a thin circle that can fit a baking sheet or pizza pan.

3. Bake the dough at 375 degrees F until golden and crisp at the edges, or for about 20 to 25 minutes.

4. Let the dough cool for a further 20 minutes or so to form a crunchy crust.

5. Top the pizza crust as you like and then return the crust to the oven for a few more minutes to cook the toppings.

Nutritional information per serving: Calories 172.6, Carbs 4g, Protein 7.7g, Fat 14.6g

Low Carb Pizza Crust

Serves 4-6

Ingredients

For crust

½ teaspoon garlic powder

½ teaspoon dried basil

½ teaspoon dried oregano

⅔ cup almond meal

1 egg

3 tablespoons cream cheese

1 ½ cups shredded mozzarella

For topping

Choice of vegetables, cheese, meat

Pizza sauce (pasta sauce)

Directions

1. Preheat your oven to 425 degrees F.

2. In a heat safe bowl, microwave the cream cheese and the mozzarella for about 35 seconds, or until soft.

3. Add in the egg, basil, oregano and almond meal and mix well to form dough ball.

4. Press the dough into a square or a circle and put it on a baking sheet lined with parchment paper; and sprayed with a thin layer of coconut oil or olive oil layer.

5. Season the surface of the pizza crust with basil and garlic salt. Get a fork and poke a few holes on the crust to help release air while baking.

6. Bake for approximately 8 to 10 minutes, and then broil for another 1 to 2 minutes.

7. Top the pizza crust with pizza sauce and other favorite toppings and then return into the oven.

8. Bake until cheese is melted and bubbly or for a further 4 to 5 minutes.

Nutritional information per serving: Calories 103, Carbs 6.3g, Protein 4.7g, Fat 6.6g

Zero Carb Pizza Crust

Serves 4

Ingredients

1/4 teaspoon pepper

1/4 teaspoon salt

1 tablespoon Italian seasoning

1/2 cup cheddar cheese, shredded

1/2 cup Parmesan cheese

1 lb ground chicken

Directions

1. Get a parchment paper and a tin foil and then line your baking sheet.

2. Into the chicken, add in cheddar and Parmesan cheeses along with the spices, and then mix well.

3. Make a log shape from the dough and put it on the prepared baking sheet. Spread the dough evenly to the shape of a pizza crust.

4. Bake the dough at 425 degrees F for approximately 35 minutes or until you get a crispy crust.

5. You can brush with olive oil as soon as you remove the crust from the oven and then top, as you like. Return to the oven and bake for a further 10 to 12 minutes.

Nutritional information per serving: Calories 296, Carbs 2g, Protein 29g, Fat 2g

Fathead Pizza Crust

Serves 1

Ingredients

Sea salt

Garlic powder

1 teaspoon xanthan gum

1 egg

2 tablespoons cream cheese, cubed

3/4 cup almond flour

1 1/2 cups shredded mozzarella

Directions

1. Preheat your oven to 425 degrees F. Stir together garlic powder, almond floor, xanthan gum and salt in a medium bowl.

2. Place the cheeses in a heat-safe bowl and heat for about 1 1/2 minutes.

3. Stir the cheese for half a minute then add in the egg and almond flour mixture. In case it is too stringy, microwave it for about 30 seconds or so.

4. Wet your hands and then make the dough into 5 balls. Place them, on a baking sheet lined with parchment paper.

5. Spread the balls with your wet hands to ensure they are thin enough as it helps them crisp up quickly.

6. Using a fork, poke the crust all over and then bake for around 8 minutes.

7. Use the fork to poke down bubbles and then cook until the crust has browned; let's say for another 4 minutes.

8. Finally spread with your preferred topping and then enjoy!

Nutritional information per serving: Calories 192, Carbs 4g, Protein 12g, Fat 15g

Gluten Free Tart Crust

Serves: 2

Ingredients

1 large egg

2 tablespoons coconut oil

½ teaspoon Celtic sea salt

2 cups blanched almond flour

Directions

1. Put salt and almond flour in a blender or food processor and pulse for a few seconds.

2. Add in the egg and coconut then pulse until you have a ball.

3. Press the dough into a 9-inch tart pan and add in pie fillings that you like.

4. Bake the pie until ready to serve.

Nutritional information per serving: Calories 152, Carbs 0.56g, Protein 1.6g, Fat 16.5g

Pizza Bread Crust

Serves 8

Ingredients

50g sun dried tomatoes

Pinch of pepper

4 tablespoons extra-virgin olive oil, cold-pressed

100g flax seeds

200g sunflower seeds

Pinch of organic salt or sea salt

Wild garlic, fresh

Directions

1. Pre-soak the sunflower seeds for more than 4 hours or overnight.

2. In a mixer, add in flax seeds and grind them until you have fine-grained powder.

3. Remove the sunflower seeds from the water and process them in a mixer for a few seconds.

4. Transfer everything into a bowl and knead the dough using your fingers to create the desired consistency. You can also add in some olive oil or distilled water.

5. Create a few pizza breads or pizza crusts and place them in a dehydrator or oven overnight for at least 12 hours.

6. Once ready, serve add your toppings, bake your pizza and serve.

Nutritional information per serving: Calories 281, Carbs 8.9g, Protein 7.6g, Fat 26g

Bagels/Donuts

Mozzarella Dough Bagels

Serves: 6

Ingredients

1 teaspoon baking powder

1 medium egg

2 tablespoons cream cheese full fat

85g almond meal/flour

170g pre-shredded/grated mozzarella cheese

Pinch salt

Directions

1. Combine the cream cheese, almond flour and mozzarella cheese in a heat safe bowl.

2. Microwave the mixture on high setting for approximately 1 minute, stir and microwave for 30 more seconds.

3. Add in salt, baking powder and egg along with preferred flavorings; mix until well combined.

4. Divide the bagel dough into 6 equal parts and then roll each into a ball and then into a cylinder.

5. Fold the ends of these cylinders to form a circle. Now squeeze the ends of the dough together to make a bagel.

6. Put the bagels on a baking tray and then top with sesame seeds.

7. Bake the bagels at 425 degrees F until golden brown or for approximately 15 minutes.

Nutritional information per serving: Calories 203, Carbs 4g, Protein 11g, Fat 16.8g

Easy Keto Bagel

Serves 6

Ingredients

2 eggs

1/2 cup grated Parmesan

1 cup shredded mozzarella or cheddar cheese

2 tablespoons everything bagel seasoning

Directions

1. Preheat your oven to 373 degrees F.

2. Mix together egg and shredded cheese in a bowl until the two ingredients are blended.

3. Divide the mixture into 6 equal portions and then press them into a greased donut-cooking pan.

4. Sprinkle the top of the cheese and egg mixture with the seasoning and put in the oven.

5. Bake at 375 degrees F or until the cheese melts and creates a light brown crust, or for approximately 15 to 20 minutes.

Nutritional information per serving: Calories 218, Carbs 5g, Protein 14g, Fat 16g

Keto Bagels

Serves: 6

Ingredients

1 teaspoon baking powder

1 large egg

3/4 cup almond flour

1 ounce cream cheese

1 1/2 cups shredded mozzarella cheese

Seasoning of choice

Directions

1. Preheat your oven to 400 degrees F. Meanwhile line your baking sheet with parchment.

2. In a heat safe bowl, mix cream cheese and the mozzarella and then microwave on high setting for 30 seconds.

3. Stir with a fork for a moment and then microwave for a further 30 seconds until the cheeses have completely melted.

4. Add in the egg, almond flour and baking powder and then mix with a fork. Mix again with a spatula or your hands until you have dough of uniform appearance.

5. Divide the dough into 6 equally sized balls and then use your hands to roll each of them into a log.

6. Make a circle and put the dough onto the parchment paper. Repeat with the rest of the balls.

7. Lightly coat each of the dough with water so that the seasoning can easily stick.

8. Season well while pressing down on the dough using your fingers. Bake the bagels for approximately 12 to 14 minutes.

Nutritional information per serving: Calories 191, Carbs 4g, Protein 10g, Fat 15g

Keto Sesame Bagels

Serves: 6

Ingredients

1/4 cup sesame seeds

1 large egg, lightly beaten

1 tablespoon baking powder

1 1/2 cups finely ground blanched almond flour

1 ounce cream cheese, cubed

1 1/2 cups shredded part skim mozzarella

Directions

1. Preheat your oven to 350 degrees F. Meanwhile line your baking sheet with parchment.

2. Place the mozzarella cheese in a heat safe bowl and then add in the cream cheese.

3. Microwave the ingredients for 30 seconds, stir and then microwave for another 30 seconds.

4. Stir a second time and then add in baking powder and almond flour. Stir to blend.

5. Add in the egg and mix well using a rubber spatula and then with your hands. Do everything fast before the dough cools down!

6. Divide the dough in 6 portions and roll each of them in 7-inch log. Then press the ends of the log to form a bagel.

7. Dip the tops of the bagel dough in sesame seeds and then arrange them on the lined baking sheet.

8. Bake the bagels for 15 to 17 minutes, or until golden brown and fragrant.

Nutritional information per serving: Calories 281, Carbs 8g, Protein 15g, Fat 22g

Low-Carb Bagels

Serves 8

Ingredients

1 tablespoon baking powder

2 large eggs

1 3/4 cups almond flour

2 ounces cream cheese

3 cups mozzarella cheese shredded

3 tablespoons everything seasoning, optional

Directions

1. Preheat the oven to 350 degrees F. Meanwhile, line a baking sheet using parchment paper.

2. Into a large heat-safe bowl, mix cream cheese and mozzarella cheese and then microwave the mixture until the cheese has melted, or for approximately 2 minutes.

3. Remove the bowl from the microwave and stir using a fork until the mixture has fully blended.

4. Add in baking powder, egg and almond flour, and then stir to incorporate the eggs and the flour into the cheese. In case the dough is sticky, knead it using your hands.

5. Cut the dough into 8 equal parts, and shape each of the segments into a doughnut.

6. Put the doughnut-shaped dough on the lined baking sheet, and bake for approximately 15 minutes.

7. If need be, broil for about 1 minute or so just to brown the top of the Keto bagel. You can garnish with preferred topping if you like it.

Nutritional information per serving: Calories 318, Carbs 7.5g, Protein 16.3g, Fat 26.6g

Fathead Bagel

Serves 4-6

Ingredients

2 large eggs

2 ounces cream cheese

2 1/2 cups shredded mozzarella

1 tablespoon baking powder

1 3/4 cups almond flour

Sesame seeds

Directions

1. Preheat your oven to 400 degrees F. Get some parchment paper and line your baking sheet.

2. In a bowl, combine baking powder and almond flour and set the mixture aside.

3. Put cream cheese and the mozzarella in a bowl and microwave the cheeses until fully melted or for approximately 2 minutes, ensuring that you stir after a minute.

4. Into the melted cheese, add in the egg and almond flour mixture and then mix everything with your hands until fully blended.

5. Ensure the dough is hot throughout the mixing process even though it is very sticky.

6. Divide the dough into 6 portions and roll each of them into a rope. Then mold each of the rope into a bagel

7. Top the bagels with sesame seeds if you like. Bake them for about 10 to 14 minutes at 400 degrees F.

8. Allow to cool for a couple of minutes and then remove from the oven. Serve hot!

Nutritional information per serving; Calories 440, Carbs 3g, Protein 42g, Fat 31g

Muffins

Keto Egg Muffins

Serves 2

Ingredients

1/4 cup grated cheddar cheese

2 tablespoons water

2 tablespoons heavy whipping cream

1 large egg, free-range or organic

1/4 teaspoon baking soda

1/4 cup flax meal

1/4 cup almond flour

Himalayan salt

For filling:

1 teaspoon Dijon mustard

2 slices cheddar cheese

2 tablespoons cream cheese

1 tablespoon ghee

2 large eggs, free range or organic

Salt

Pepper

2 cups greens, optional

4 slices crisped up bacon, optional

Directions

1. Mix all the dry ingredients in a bowl. Add the egg, water and cream, and use a fork to mix.

2. Grate the cheese, and add into the mixture. Mix well and put the new mixture into ramekins. Microwave the contents for 60-90 seconds.

3. Fry the eggs using ghee and cook until the egg white is opaque and the yolk is runny. Using some pepper and salt, season the dish and then remove from heat.

4. Now cut the muffins in half and then spread the cheese on the inside of each of them. Top each half with mustard, egg and cheese.

5. You can serve with the greens and bacon if you like it that way. Serve and enjoy!

Nutritional information per serving: Calories 626, Carbs 9.4g, Protein 26.5g, Fat 54.6g

Almond and Coconut Muffin

Serves 1

Ingredients

1 teaspoon extra virgin olive oil

1 large egg

1/8 teaspoon salt

1/4 teaspoon baking powder

1/2 teaspoon cinnamon

1 teaspoon sucralose based sweetener

1/3 tablespoon organic coconut flour, high fiber

2 tablespoons almond meal flour

1 tablespoon sour cream

Directions

1. Into a coffee mug, add in all the dry ingredients and stir to incorporate.

2. Add in oil and egg, and mix well.

3. Microwave for about 60 seconds then remove the muffin from the cup using a knife.

4. Slice, put some butter and serve.

Nutritional information per serving; Calories 231, Carbs 3.7g, Protein 9.7g, Fat 19.8g

Salmon & Cream Cheese Mug Muffin

Serves 2

Ingredients

2 tablespoons water

2 tablespoons cream or coconut milk

1 large egg, free-range or organic

¼ teaspoon baking soda

¼ cup flax meal

¼ cup almond flour

Pinch of salt

2 tablespoons spring onion or chives, freshly chopped

60g smoked salmon

2 dollops full-fat sour cream or cream cheese, optional

Directions

1. In a small bowl, put all the dry ingredients and mix well.

2. Add in the egg, cream and water and combine using a fork.

3. Finely chop the chives and slice the smoked salmon. Add salmon and chives to the mixture and mix well.

4. Microwave for 60-90 seconds on high, and then top with cream cheese and serve.

Nutritional information per serving: Carbs 9.5g, Protein 17.2g, Fat 32.3g

Avocado & Bacon Muffins

Makes 12

Ingredients

Salt & pepper to taste

1/2 teaspoon baking soda

1/2 cup coconut flour

1 cup coconut milk

2 cups avocado

4 eggs

6 short cut bacon rashers

1 small onion

Directions

1. Preheat the oven to 350 degrees F and then use coconut oil to grease 12 muffin cups.

2. Finely dice the bacon and onion and brown these in a frying pan.

3. Meanwhile, use a fork to mix the eggs and avocado together and then stir in the milk.

4. Add in salt and pepper, baking soda and coconut floor and mix well ensuring that you break up all lumps.

5. Fold through the 3 quarters of the onion and cooked bacon mixture.

6. Divide the mixture between the 12 muffin cups and top with the reserved onion and bacon.

7. Bake in the preheated oven for about 20 minutes; and cool allow to cool before removing the muffins from the muffin tins.

8. Serve immediately or alternatively keep chilled in the fridge for outdoor breakfasts.

Nutritional information per serving: Calories 105, Carbs 4g, Protein 5g, Fat 8.4g

Low Carb English Muffin

Serves: 2

Ingredients

1 egg beaten

1 tablespoon almond milk, unsweetened

1/2 teaspoon baking powder

1/8 teaspoon salt

2 tablespoons almond flour

1 tablespoon butter

2 tablespoons almond or cashew butter, unsweetened

Directions

1. Coat the ramekins with cooking spray or olive oil and then add cashew butter and butter to the dish.

2. Microwave the mixture for half a minute and combine until well incorporated. Set it aside to cool down.

3. Meanwhile, whisk together baking powder, salt and almond flour in a small dish. Add in the egg and milk to the mixture and stir until well blended.

4. Pour the mixture into the ramekin with the butter almond mixture. Stir to mix.

5. Microwave the batter for about 2 minutes and then let it cool down.

6. Finally remove the muffin from the ramekin and serve.

Nutritional information per serving: Calories 222, Carbs 5g, Protein 7g, Fat 20g

Lemon Poppy-seed Muffins

Serves 12

Ingredients

25 drops liquid stevia

1 teaspoon vanilla extract

3 tablespoons lemon juice

Zest of 2 lemons

3 large eggs

1/4 cup heavy cream

1/4 cup salted butter, melted

1 teaspoon baking powder

1/3 cup erythritol

1/4 cup golden flax seed meal

3/4 cup blanched almond flour

2 tablespoons poppy seeds

Directions

1. Preheat an oven to 350 degrees F; and then mix the poppy seeds, erythritol, flax seed meal and almond flour using a fork.

2. Stir in the eggs, melted butter and heavy cream and continue to beat until you have a smooth consistency. Make sure that there are no visible lumps left in your batter.

3. Add in vanilla extract, liquid stevia, lemon juice, lemon zest and baking powder and mix.

4. Subdivide the batter into 12 cupcake molds. You can use ordinary muffin pan or silicon cupcake molds.

5. Bake for about 18-20 minutes or until they turn somehow brown. You can bake on the higher side in order to achieve a better crust.

6. Once done, remove from the oven and let it cool on the counter for about 10 minutes.

7. Finally slice and serve, preferably with a half pad of butter between the muffins.

Nutritional information per serving: Calories 129.8, Carbs 3.3g, Protein 4.04g, Fat 11.7g

One-Minute Keto Muffins

Serves 1

Ingredients

Pinch of baking soda

2 teaspoons coconut flour

1 large egg

Pinch of salt

Directions

1. Using butter or coconut oil, grease a ramekin dish and set aside.

2. Mix all the ingredients in a mug and whisk them using a fork to remove all lumps.

3. Pour this into the greased ramekin and microwave on high for about 1 minute. If need be, you can also bake in a preheated oven at 400 degrees F for about 12 minutes.

4. Cut the muffin in half and serve.

Nutritional information per serving; Calories 113, Carbs 5g, Protein 7g, Fat 6g

Keto Bread

Blueberry Muffin

> To make 12 deep muffins
> x 3 Recipe
> Bake at 180°C for at least 30 mins or until golden brown

Serves: 6

Ingredients

¼ cup fresh blueberries *(use 1 cup)*

1 egg, room temperature

2 tablespoons coconut oil, melted

½ cup coconut milk, full fat

2 tablespoons sweetener

⅛ teaspoon baking soda

1 cup blanched almond flour

Pinch of salt

Optional

1/4 cup chopped nuts

1/3 cup of dark chocolate chips

1 teaspoon vanilla extract

Directions

1. Preheat the oven to about 350 degrees F and then get a non-stick muffin pan or instead line a muffin tin with muffin cups.

Keto Bread

2. Combine the salt, baking soda and almond flour then whisk together egg, coconut oil, coconut milk and honey in a separate bowl.

3. Mix the dry and wet ingredients together using a rubber spatula taking care not to over mix.

4. Slowly fold the blueberries into the batter. Spoon the batter into the muffin pan or muffin tin to the top.

5. Bake for about 20 to 25 minutes. Insert a toothpick into the muffin and if it comes out clean, they are ready.

6. Put the pan onto a wire rack for the muffins to cool down.

Nutritional information per serving: Calories 230, Carbs 7g, Protein 1g, Fat 27g

[Handwritten note: Add vanilla/almond extract.]

Cookies

Thick and Fudgy Brownie Cookies

Serves: 10 cookies

Ingredients

1/2 cup sugar free chocolate chips

Pinch of salt

1 teaspoon vanilla extract

1 teaspoon baking soda

1/2 cup cocoa powder

2 eggs beaten

3/4 cup xylitol

1/3 cup coconut flour

3/4 cup butter melted

Directions

1. Preheat the oven to 350 degrees F and then line your baking sheet.

2. Mix together coconut flour, melted butter and xylitol in a large bowl. Add in beaten eggs and use an electric mixer to mix.

3. Add in baking soda, cocoa powder, salt and vanilla extract. Mix the ingredients with the electric mixer.

4. Using a rubber spatula, add in the chocolate chips and fold into the batter.

5. Scoop out about 10 cookies using a large cookie scoop.

6. Press about 3 or 4 chocolate chips on the cookies and place them in the hot oven.

7. Bake the cookies for approximately 13 minutes. Once cooked through, remove from the oven and let them cool.

8. Remove from the baking sheet and serve.

Nutritional information per serving: Calories 208, Carbs 12.9g, protein 3.7g, Fat 20g

Snowball Cookies

Serves 16

Ingredients

1/2 cup powdered erythritol

1/2 cup coconut flour

1 cup walnuts

40 to 50 drops liquid stevia extract

1/2 teaspoon vanilla extract

1 large egg

1/2 cup softened butter

Directions

1. Preheat your oven to 300 degrees F. Get parchment paper and line two baking sheets; set aside.

2. In a bowl, beat vanilla, egg, butter and Stevia until blended.

3. Put walnuts in a blender and pulse until ground. Add them into the bowl.

4. Add in ¼ cup of erythritol and coconut flour and stir until mixed.

Keto Bread

5. Whisk the dry mixture into the wet ingredients in two batches. Stir everything until you get soft dough.

6. Foam 16 balls from the dough and then roll each in the remaining ground erythritol.

7. Put the balls on a baking sheet and bake for approximately 30 minutes.

8. Let them cool for another 5 to 20 minutes while still in the pan, and then serve.

Nutritional information per serving: Calories 115, Carbs 5g, Protein 2.5g, Fat 7.5g

Keto Chocolate Chunk Cookies

Serves 8

Ingredients

1 large egg

1/4 cup erythritol

1/2 teaspoon baking powder

10 drops liquid stevia

5 bars Chocó-perfection cocoa bar

2 teaspoons vanilla extract

8 tablespoons unsalted butter

2 tablespoons psyllium husk

2 tablespoons coconut flour

3 tablespoons whey protein, unflavored

1 cup almond flour

Directions

1. Preheat the oven to 350 degrees F.

2. Mix together whey protein, baking powder, psyllium husk, coconut flour and almond flour in a bowl.

3. Beat butter until golden then add in stevia and erythritol and continue to beat.

4. Add the vanilla and egg mixture and beat to fully incorporate. Sift the coconut and almond flour mixture over the butter mixture and combine well.

5. Now chop the 5 bars of cocoa into chunks and mix into the dough. Roll the dough out into a log look-like and cut into 16 slices.

6. Roll the dough into balls, put on a silpat and press using the base of a mason jar.

7. Bake for around 12-15 minutes and then serve when cool.

Nutritional information per serving: Calories 118.4g, Carbs 4.4g, Protein 2.6g, Fat 10.8g

Easy Almond Thins

Serves 9

Ingredients

1 tablespoon slivered almonds, chopped

1/2 teaspoon almond extract

1/2 cup almond flour

1/3 cup coconut sugar

1 egg white

Directions

1. Preheat your oven to 300 degrees F and then line a baking dish with parchment paper.

2. In a bowl, whisk the egg white, almond extract and coconut sugar. Fold in almond flour and mix to incorporate.

3. Spread the batter into 8x8 baking dish, and sprinkle almonds over the top. Press the batter down lightly.

4. Bake for 25 minutes, or until brown. Transfer the cookies to a cooling rack by lifting them using the parchment paper.

5. Cool for about 1 hour and then serve.

Nutritional information per serving: Calories 67, Carbs 7g, Protein 2g, Fat 4g

Keto No Bake Cookies

Serves: 18 cookies

Ingredients

1 tablespoon cocoa powder

4 drops of vanilla stevia

1 cup all natural shredded coconut, unsweetened

2/3 cup all natural nut butter

2 tablespoons real butter

Directions

1. Melt butter in microwave-safe bowl and then stir in preferred nut butter until smooth.

2. In case you want to use cocoa powder, add it in, along with coconut and stevia. Mix to combine.

3. Scoop 2-inch spoonfuls of the mixture and put on a sheet pan and keep chilled for about 5 to 10 minutes.

4. Store in a sealed bag refrigerated.

Nutritional information per serving: Calories 94, Carbs 2.6g, Protein 0.3g, Fat 9.5g

Chocolate Coconut Cookies

Serves: 12

Ingredients

½ cup of dark chocolate chips

½ teaspoon of sea salt

¼ teaspoon of baking soda

¼ cup of cocoa powder

3 tablespoons of sifted coconut flour

1-tablespoon pure vanilla extract

2 large eggs

2/3 cup of coconut sugar

1/3 cup non melted of coconut oil

Directions

1. Preheat the oven to 350 degrees F.

2. In a mixing bowl, beat the sugar and coconut oil and then add the eggs and keep on beating on medium speed until it's well mixed. Stir in the vanilla extract.

3. Follow with the coconut flour, baking soda and cocoa powder and the salt and stir until it is well incorporated.

4. Lightly coat a baking sheet with coconut oil or instead line it with a parchment paper. Drop spoonfuls of the butter on the baking sheet about 2 inches apart.

5. Bake the cookies for about 12 minutes. Allow to cool before removing from baking sheet.

Nutritional information per serving: Calories 90, Carbs 7g, Protein 0.8g, Fat 7g

Keto Mug Bread

Serves: 1

Ingredients

1 tablespoon olive oil

1 egg

1/2 teaspoon baking powder

4 tablespoons almond meal/flour

Pinch of salt

Directions

1. Mix all the ingredients in a mug using a fork until well incorporated.

2. Once well mixed, microwave the batter on high for about 60 seconds. Tap the top of the mug bread to ensure it is cooked through, if not done microwave for an additional 20 to 30 seconds.

3. Turn the mug upside down to remove the bread, and allow it to cool.

4. Slice and serve, or instead toast it for a crispier texture. You can serve it alone or as a sandwich bun.

Nutritional information per serving; Calories 278, Carbs 2.6g, Protein 10g, Fat 15.5g

Crockpot Zucchini Bread

Serves 10 slices

Ingredients

1/2 teaspoon vanilla extract

1/4 cup water

1/4 cup coconut oil

3 large eggs

1/4 teaspoon nutmeg

1/2 teaspoon ginger

2 teaspoons cinnamon

2 teaspoons baking powder

1/4 cup egg white protein powder, unflavored

1/2 cup Swerve Sweetener

2/3 cup shredded coconut

1 1/3 cups almond flour

1/2 teaspoon salt

½ cup chopped nuts

2 1/2 cups shredded zucchini

Directions

1. Put the zucchini in a sieve over a sink or bowl. Season with salt and then allow it to drain for about 1 hour.

2. Squeeze out as much fluid as possible and then set aside. Meanwhile grease your crock pot's insert.

3. Whisk together shredded coconut, almond flour, nutmeg, ginger, cinnamon, baking powder, protein powder and a sweetener in a large bowl.

4. Stir in melted butter, eggs, zucchini, vanilla extract and water until well combined.

5. Spread the mixture in a Crockpot, cover and cook for 2 ½ to 3 hours on low heat setting.

6. Let this cool inside the Crockpot and then slice and enjoy.

Nutritional information per serving: Calories 238, Carbs 6.91g, Protein 8.95g, Fat 20.22g

Cheesy Cauliflower Garlic Bread

Serves 8 slices

Ingredients

1/4 cup chopped fresh basil

2 cloves garlic, minced

1/2 teaspoon pepper

1/2 teaspoon salt

3 tablespoons coconut flour

2 cups shredded mozzarella, divided

2 large eggs

12 ounces cauliflower florets

Directions

1. Grease a Crockpot and set aside. Chop the cauliflower in a food processor until you have a rice-like consistency. Transfer to a large bowl.

2. Stir in pepper, salt, coconut flour, eggs and a cup of shredded cheese. Stir this mixture to blend it fully.

3. Press the mixture into the bottom of the greased Crockpot, and then sprinkle the remaining cheese along with garlic.

4. Once done, cook on high until the edges are crisp and browned and the cheese has melted, or for about 2-4 hours.

5. Cut the bread into slices and remove from the Crockpot. Sprinkle with basil and enjoy.

Nutritional information per serving: Calories 224, Carbs: 5.63g, Protein: 15.29g, Fat: 14.95g

Low Carb Quick Bread

Serves: 1

Ingredients

1 egg

Pinch salt

½ teaspoon baking powder

3 tablespoons almond flour

2 tablespoons unsalted butter

Directions

1. In a heat safe bowl, heat 2 tablespoons of unsalted butter until melted. Swirl the melted butter in the sides of the bowl to coat, and let them cool for some time.

2. Add in baking powder, almond flour and salt. Mix or whisk until blended together.

3. Add in the egg and mix until the egg has fully blended with the batter.

4. Cook the batter in the microwave for approximately 1 minute 30 seconds, and then transfer to a cooling rack for a few minutes.

5. Once cool to handle, cut the bread into slices.

Nutritional information per serving; Calories 387, Carbs 5g, Protein 10g, Fat 37g

Broccoli & Cheddar Keto Bread

Serves: 10 slices

Ingredients

2 teaspoons baking powder

3 1/2 tablespoons coconut flour

3/4 cup fresh raw broccoli florets chopped

1 cup shredded cheddar cheese

5 eggs beaten

1 teaspoon salt

Directions

1. Preheat your oven to 350 degrees F. Coat a spray loaf using cooking spray.

2. In a medium bowl combine all the ingredients and once done, transfer them to a loaf pan.

3. Bake the mixture until puffed and golden, or for approximately 30 to 35 minutes.

4. Now slice and enjoy.

Nutritional information per serving: Calories 90, Carbs 2g, Protein 6g, Fat 6g

Conclusion

We have come to the end of the book. Thank you for reading and congratulations for reading until the end.

If you found the book valuable, can you recommend it to others? One way to do that is to post a review on Amazon.

Don't forget to leave a review for this book on Amazon!

Do You Like My Book & Approach To Publishing?

If you like my writing and style and would love the ease of learning literally everything you can get your hands on from Fantonpublishers.com, I'd really need you to do me either of the following favors.

1: First, I'd Love It If You Leave a Review of This Book on Amazon.

2: Check Out My Other Keto Diet Books

KETOGENIC DIET: Keto Diet Made Easy: Beginners Guide on How to Burn Fat Fast With the Keto Diet (Including 100+ Recipes That You Can Prepare Within 20 Minutes)- New Edition

KETOGENIC DIET: Ketogenic Diet Recipes That You Can Prepare Using 7 Ingredients and Less in Less Than 30 Minutes

Ketogenic Diet: With A Sustainable Twist: Lose Weight Rapidly With Ketogenic Diet Recipes You Can Make Within 25 Minutes

Ketogenic Diet: Keto Diet Breakfast Recipes

Fat Bombs: Keto Fat Bombs: 50+ Savory and Sweet Ketogenic Diet Fat Bombs That You MUST Prepare Before Any Other!

[Snacks: Keto Diet Snacks: 50+ Savory and Sweet Ketogenic Diet Snacks That You MUST Prepare Before Any Other!](#)

[Desserts: Keto Diet Desserts: 50+ Savory and Sweet Ketogenic Diet Desserts That You MUST Prepare Before Any Other!](#)

[Ketogenic Diet: Ketogenic Diet Lunch and Dinner Recipes](#)

[Ketogenic Diet: Keto Diet Cookbook For Vegetarians](#)

[Ketogenic Diet: Ketogenic Slow Cooker Cookbook: Keto Slow Cooker Recipes That You Can Prepare Using 7 Ingredients Or Less](#)

Note: This list may not represent all my Keto diet books. You can check the full list by visiting my [Author Profile](#): [amazon.com/author/fantonpublishers](#) or my website [http://www.fantonpublishers.com](#)

Get updates when we publish any book on the Ketogenic diet: [http://bit.ly/2fantonpubketo](#)

Closely related to the keto diet is intermittent fasting. I also publish books on Intermittent Fasting.

One of the books is shown below:

Intermittent Fasting: A Complete Beginners Guide to Intermittent Fasting For Weight Loss, Increased Energy, and A Healthy Life

Get updates when we publish any book on intermittent fasting: http://bit.ly/2fantonbooksIF

To get a list of all my other books, please check out fantonpublishers.com, my author profile or let me send you the list by requesting them below: http://bit.ly/2fantonpubnewbooks

3: Let's Get In Touch

Antony

Website: http://www.fantonpublishers.com/

Email: Support@fantonpublishers.com

Twitter: https://twitter.com/FantonPublisher

Facebook Page: https://www.facebook.com/Fantonpublisher/

My Ketogenic Diet Books Page: https://www.facebook.com/pg/Fast-Keto-Meals-336338180266944

Private Facebook Group For Readers: https://www.facebook.com/groups/FantonPublishers/

Pinterest: https://www.pinterest.com/fantonpublisher/

4: Grab Some Freebies On Your Way Out; Giving Is Receiving, Right?

I gave you 2 freebies at the start of the book, one on general life transformation and one about the Ketogenic diet. Grab them here if you didn't grab them earlier.

Ketogenic Diet Freebie: http://bit.ly/2fantonpubketo

5 Pillar Life Transformation Checklist: http://bit.ly/2fantonfreebie

5: Suggest Topics That You'd Love Me To Cover To Increase Your Knowledge Bank.

I am looking forward to seeing your suggestions and insights; you could even suggest improvements to this book. Simply send me a message on Support@fantonpublishers.com.

PSS: Let Me Also Help You Save Some Money!

If you are a heavy reader, have you considered subscribing to Kindle Unlimited? You can read this and millions of other books for just $9.99 a month)! You can check it out by searching for Kindle Unlimited on Amazon!

Printed in Great Britain
by Amazon